the humorous
GOLF POETRY
of Tom Edwards

Raven Tree Press
Green Bay, Wisconsin

Raven Tree Press

Copyright © 2001 by Tom Edwards
All rights reserved
Manufactured in the United States of America
First Printing, May, 2001
06 05 04 03 02 01 9 8 7 6 5 4 3 2 1

Edited by Amy Crane Johnson
Book Design by Laura Diedrick
Jacket Design by Laura Diedrick
Illustrated by Claude Schneider

Printed in the United States of America

For information contact:
Raven Tree Press, LLC
130 E. Walnut – Suite 410
Green Bay, WI 54301
toll free 877-256-0579
www.raventreepress.com

Publisher's Cataloging-in-Publication
(Provided by Quality Books, Inc.)

Edwards, Tom (Thomas M.)
    The humorous golf poetry of Tom Edwards. – 1st ed.

    p. cm.
    LCCN 2001116674
    ISBN 0-9701107-1-5

    1. Golf–Poetry. 2. Golf–Humor.   I. Title.

PS3555.D985H86 2001   811'.6
                QBI01-700461

This book is printed on acid-free paper.

FIRST EDITION

Acknowledgments

Thanks to the following publications, where many of these poems (sometimes in earlier versions) first appeared or were awarded prizes.

Putting Resurrection –*Mid-South Golfer*. Golfing Friendships –*Mid-South Golfer; Fentress Courier; T. R.'s Zine Magazine*. Billy Sinclair –*Standard of Roane County; Metrolina Golf Magazine; Loudon County Independent; Fairfield Glade Bulletin; Standard of Morgan County; Fairfield Mountain Breeze; Mid-South Golfer*. Golfing Hopes –*Fairfield Glade Sun; T. R.'s Zine Magazine; Fairfield Mountain Breeze*. Putting Goals –*Standard of Morgan County*. Wishing On A Tee –*Fairfield Glade Sun; Putnam County Star*. Golfing Smiles –*Mid-South Golfer; T. R.'s Zine Magazine*. Hit And Quit Golf –*Mid-South Golfer; Standard of Morgan County*. The Final Resting Place –*Morgan County Times; Loudon County Independent; Putnam County Star; Clinton Courier-News; Mid-South Golfer; Standard of Morgan County; T. R's Zine Magazine*. A Golfer's Baby –*Golf West Magazine; Arizona Golfer; Mid-South Golfer; "Light Verse Award," ByLine Magazine*. Long And Wrong –*Fairfield Glade Bulletin; Putnam County Beacon News-Journal; Cumberland Journal; Fairfield Glade Sun; Cumberland Times; Golfer's Tee Time*. A Change Of Heart –*Southern Visions Poetry Chapbook; Rockwood Times; Fairfield Harbor Beacon; Roane County Times; Fairfield Mountain Breeze; Fore-Golf in the Upper Cumberlands; Indianapolis Tri-County Weekly; Golfer's Tee Times; Standard of Morgan County; Mid-South Golfer; "Humorous Poem Award," ByLine Magazine*. A Putting Prayer –*Fairfield Glade Bulletin; Standard of Morgan County; Mid-South Golfer; "Four Line Rhymed Poem Award," ByLine Magazine*. Golf Ball Epitaph –*Fairfield Glade Sun; Fairfield Mountain Breeze*. Golf Score Epitaph –*East Tennessee Golf News*. Golfer, Spare That Tree –*Cumberland Times*. Do Not Putt Gentle Against The Grain –*Fairfield Glade Bulletin; Fore-Golf in the Upper Cumberlands; Cumberland Times; "Poem In Formal Structure Award," ByLine Magazine*. The Lost Ball (Twinkle, Tinkle) –*Crossville Citizens' Press Box; Loudon County Independent; Morgan County Times; Fentress Courier; Mid-South Golfer*. The Driver And The Ball –*Fairfield Glade Sun; Farragut Press Enterprise; The Worm Burner; Knoxville News-Sentinel; Fairfield Glade Bulletin; Morgan County Times; Loudon County Independent; Mid-South Golfer; Standard of Morgan County; Fairfield Mountain Breeze; Clinton Courier-News; Roane County Times; Fore-Golf in the Upper Cumberlands; Cumberland Times*. A Golfing Travesty – Since There Is No Hope –*Awards: Poetry Society of Texas; Poetry Society of Tennessee; "Poem In Formal Structure Award," ByLine Magazine*. My Putt Missed Twice –*Knoxville News-Sentinel; Standard of Morgan County; Fairfield Glade Bulletin; Clinton Courier-News; Fairfield Mountain Breeze; Mid-South Golfer*. The Puttering –*Town Springs IV Anthology by Cookeville Creative Writers; Southern Visions Poetry Chapbook; Clinton Courier-News; T. R.'s Zine Magazine; Indianapolis Tri-County Weekly; Cumberland Times; Fairfield Glade Bulletin. Awards: Poetry Society of Texas; Voices International Group; Green River Writers; "Poem In Formal Structure Award." ByLine Magazine*.

Also, many thanks to Eileen Elledge, Tim Edwards, Plateau Writers Group, Cookeville Creative Writers, Thelma Johnson and Ralph Hargraves for their assistance and support.

Dedicated to my family,
especially my wife Joan,
for her patience and understanding,
my son Mike for making this book possible,
and Raven Tree Press
for the courage and wisdom
to publish this book.

Introduction

Living on a golf course does little to improve my game, but does offer considerable insight to the overwhelming need and drive for the golfer to improve their game and lower their score. This causes the agony, despair, misery, angst, frustration, grief and torment that I have detailed in this imaginative and humorous poetry.

I can draw from personal experience with errant shots, missed putts, lost golf balls and whiffs that are an integral part of my game.

I am blessed with friends, acquaintances, howdy-do-ers and golfing passers-by who share their mistakes, errors, faults, and foibles.

Yet, we keep returning to the game of golf because of the eternal promise and hope that tomorrow will be better, the next shot will be spectacular and save us, the long putt will drop and the errant ball will be found in-bounds and playable and, most important, we will forget all past travails.

GOLF — it's only a game, but a good game.

—Tom Edwards

Table of Contents

continued...

the humorous
GOLF POETRY
of Tom Edwards

Ball Bright

Ball white, ball bright,
First ball I see tonight.
I wish I might, I wish I may
Find that ball I lost today.

Sandy Sadness

To see your golf ball in a pile of sand
Just has to be the saddest scene.
If I could only take it back in hand,
I'd throw it on that nearby green.

claude Schneider

My Putt Missed Twice

(with apologies to Emily Dickinson,
My Life Closed Twice—)

My putt missed twice before it fell
From three and one-half feet.
If no mortals were there to see,
One might have cause to cheat.

So sad, so hopeless to believe,
That twice it would not fall.
Putting will never teach of heaven,
If we need curse a ball.

A Golfer's Baby

I was playing a round of golf
The day the baby came.
Both our parents were at your side,
Adding to the shame.

They reached me on the seventh green
To tell of Billy's name.
Such was my surprise and joy,
It almost put me off my game.

Chatty Golfers

Golfers who chatter
Really don't matter.
Their constant patter
Just makes us madder.

Golfing Delights

The round began in a fearful way;
Weather and forecast were the worst.
But it quickly became a glorious day,
When, somehow, I birdied the first.

Do Not Putt Gentle Against The Grain

....

(with apologies to Dylan Thomas)

Do not putt gentle against the grain;

The steel of your nerves can ne'er subside.

Play strong, strong, lest thou suffer more pain.

Thoughtless hitters seeking the great gain

Will miss that sharp break to the outside.

Do not putt gentle against the grain.

Let not the timid your scorecard stain,

Hinting a soft break to the inside.

Play strong, strong, lest thou suffer more pain.

The wretched stroke pitiless in vain

And speak nervous words 'til you decide.

Do not putt gentle against the grain.

Envision now the shot in your brain
And fearful past doubts do set aside.
Play strong, strong, lest thou suffer more pain.

The brave man perseveres in the main;
Pray inner strength in you reside.
Do not putt gentle against the grain.
Play strong, strong, lest thou suffer more pain.

Long And Wrong

No one knew his real name,
But those in golf recalled his game.
He was long and wrong—so long and wrong;
A cause for panic in golfing's throng.

Each shot soared through the airway,
And all of them missed the fairway.
He should have had a kinder fate,
But he just couldn't hit them straight.

When the ball sliced to the right,
People there would run in fright.
And when he hooked to the left side,
That crowd scrambled for a place to hide.

No one could solve the riddle
Of why the ball missed the middle.
He never scored lower than eight,
'Cause he just couldn't hit them straight.

Most struck balls were never found;
Some didn't even hit the ground.
Many were hit right up in the air,
Giving the birds a deathly scare.

His poor wife worked night and day
To pay for the balls that went astray.
He could have been a better mate
If he just would have hit them straight.

Once he hit a hapless horse
That chanced to wander near the course.
He stunned a team behind a plow
And even wobbled a Jersey cow.

He hit more cars in parking lots
With what he thought; fairly good shots.
They said his problems would abate
If he ever learned to hit them straight.

Many years later when he died,
You can imagine how everyone cried.
They would bury him in the fairway green,
A strange kind of place he had never seen.

The way they placed him was not too deft,
With legs turned right and arms turned left.
The burial plot was a figure eight,
'Cause they couldn't even bury him straight.

claude Schneider

Golfing Friendships

Golf is but a friendly game
Played with friendly folks.
But valued friendships are ne'er the same
When we ask for strokes.

The Puttering

....

(with apologies to Elizabeth Barrett Browning,
How Do I Love Thee)

How shall I putt thee? Let me count the ways.
I can putt to the depth and width and height
Of this long green as I steadily gaze
To so far a distance, one scarce can sight.

I can putt thee with the madness of rage
And stir the heated passion strong men seek.
I can putt with the wisdom of my age,
Or the humbled gentleness of the meek.

I can putt with a smile that hides the tears,
Or with the innocence from the pureness of heart.
I can putt with the vision of past fears
And ask saintly prayers to do their part.

I putt thee best when on the final roll,
The well-puttered ball does drop in the hole.

Golf Ball Epitaph

Here lies my ball.
Please let it lie!
It had the gall
To go awry.

It raised my score
For all to see,
To one and four
Instead of three.

Fate Trait

Birdies are great,
Pars will elate,
But I really hate
Another eight.

Golfer, Spare That Tree

(with apologies to George Pope Morris)

That old oak fairway tree,
Whose great trunk hides your ball,
Caused not the whiffing spree
That led to your downfall.

Golfer, forbear thy hacks,
Lest all of nature cries.
The skills that your game lacks,
Are better served with lies.

claude Schneider

Putting Goals

A putted ball
Without a goal
Will never fall
Into the hole.

Threes

(with apologies to Joyce Kilmer)

I think that I shall never see
A score as lowly as a three.

A three should be an easy score,
But for me, please add six more.

Those high scores give so much pain,
I usually pray for days of rain.

Nines are made by hacks like me,
But only pros can make a three.

Reasonable Golfing

The wisest golfers ever known
Have never thought it cheating,
To bump a ball or nudge a ball
To roll a ball or turn a ball
To balance their competing.

Lucky Shot

The shot began with a fearful slice;
A two stroke loss would be the price.
But it hit a tree and bounced in the cup
And now our team is plus two up.

The Golferman

(with apologies to Sir Izaac Walton)

Oh, the timorous golfer's life,
It is the worst of any.
'Tis void of pleasure, full of strife,
And yet beloved by many.

Putting Joys

The greatest of joys
When putting the ball,
Is the plunking noise
As you hear it fall.

A Change Of Heart

Won't you please have a change of heart
And get back into our golfing cart?
I want you to know I do regret
Saying those things that got you upset.

I didn't know you would get so miffed
When I counted aloud the times you whiffed.
And I thought it would be cute
To joke about your golfing suit.

I know my laughter sounded smart
But I'm asking for another start.
And I won't do any more snipping
About the way you do your chipping.

I won't laugh at your putting stance
If you will give me one more chance.
You know, it's hard for us to talk
When you insist you'd rather walk.

I promise I won't fault your game
Or add any more to your shame.
Won't you please have a change of heart
And get back into our golfing cart?

claude Schneider

Oliver Goldsmith On Golfing

When losing golfer stoops to folly,
And finds too late that strokes betray,
What thoughts can soothe his melancholy,
What art can wash the score away?

The only act his score to hide,
To shield the strokes from every eye,
To save repentance to every side
And save his scoring, is, to lie.

Golfing Smiles

I laughed
As I mis-hit
My golf ball.
It cracked a smile
And disappeared.

Golfing Propriety

When you're ready to hit
And the chatting won't quit
And anger is tabooed by society;

I believe you may use
Any gesture you choose
To silence them without impropriety.

Outputted

He made the putt that closed me out,
Then topped it with a victory shout.
And being a man with a lot of gall,
I gently crushed his putted ball.

Golfer John Paul

(with apologies to Mother Goose)

Golfer John Paul
Has lost his ball
And cannot seem to find it.
If he leaves it alone
It will surely come home
In someone else's pocket.

On Purchasing A Golf Ball At A Difficult Course

(with apologies to George Martin Lane)

The golfer asks, quite ill at ease,
One golf ball Sir, if you please.
The Golf Pro roars all through the hall;
You can't play here with just one ball.

A Three Or A Seven

(with apologies to William Shakespeare,
To Be Or Not To Be...)

A three, or a seven: that is the question.
Whether 'tis lower for my score to render
A shot high lofted of a safer distance,
Or smote the sphere long-placed across yon water,
And roll high near the white pole so well masted.
Play long; play short.
O, me; and by that shot hope to end
The heart-ache, and the thousand natural shocks
Golfery is heir to. 'Tis a consummation
Devoutly to be wished. Play long; play short.
Which way? Perchance to par! Aye, there's the point.
For if we bogey here, what strokes may come
When we have shuffled off to putt the further green?
This gives us pause...

Of Tree Leaves And Golf Balls

My ball likes the leaves,
And where they abound.
It hides underneath
And is rarely found.

Out Of Bounds With
Robert Frost

Whose ball this is I think I know,
Although I hoped it wasn't so.
I wish they would remove this stake;
Then all this grief I could forsake.

No one will see me stooping low
To give my ball an in-bounds throw.
If I don't give my ball a toss
I will incur a two-stroke loss.

My little ball must think it queer
For me to risk a golf career.
But between this shot and yonder lake,
Are other hazards that I fear.

If that last shot I must remake
There will be little cause to cheer,
And so many holes left to go—
And so many holes left to go.

Twilight Time On The Golf Course

It's twilight and the distant sun
Is slowly fading in the west.
The rippling waters in silence run
And birds are on their downy nest.

The gentle moo of restive cow
And katydids from trees so high,
The owls perched on leafy bough
Against the veil of darkened sky.

It's twilight and a peaceful time
With sounds and silence of nightfall.
By rights, it should be my bedtime
But I'm still looking for my ball.

On Weeding Of Putts

A putt can sometimes
Be hard to read,
When embedded
In a weed.

Growing Up

(with apologies to Edna St. Vincent Millay)

Was it for this I practiced daily
And then to hit that putt so frailly,
That now must humbly shuffle away?
I should retire and take up croquet.

Putting Kindness

It seems so cruel and inhuman
To watch the fourth putt of a man.
That ball may never find the cup;
A decent partner would pick it up.

A Golfer's Toast

Here is a toast to your golf game:
May your drives always hit the mark.
May the fairway always follow your ball.
May the greens always run true.
And may your score always
Equal your expectations.

Billy Sinclair

This is the tale of Billy Sinclair
And of the day he met his end.
He hit a drive straight up in the air,
But failed to watch the ball descend.

When he doffed his cap to honor the cheer,
The ball came down upon his head.
It struck with a thud that all could hear,
Which, of course, did leave him quite dead.

Golf Widow Lament

(with apologies to Samuel Hoffenstein)

When you're out golfing, I'm restless, lonely
Wretched, bored, dejected; only
Here's the rub, my darling golfer dear,
I feel the same when you are here.

A Time To Golf

It's best to golf
When morning's light
Resounds across the deep,
And the lilting song
Of the robin bright
Hushes the rocks to sleep.

Before the bright red sun
In the blaze of noon
Is bathed in crumbling dew,
Before the Ranger yells out
In a blaring shout,
You're two holes behind!
Get a move on you!

Putting Resurrection

Dear golfer, bear not a saddened heart,
And receive the joy we can impart.
Put back the putt that did not fall,
And take a "gimmee" from us all.

The Driver And The Ball

(with apologies to Henry Wadsworth
Longfellow, The Arrow and the Song)

I hit a golf ball into the air;
It fell to earth I knew not where.
For, so swiftly it sliced, the eye
Could not follow across the sky.

I threw my driver into the air;
Where it fell to earth, I did not care.
With every shot a slice or dub,
Why would I want to keep that club?

Some time later having lost a stroke,
I found the driver still unbroke.
But, alas, to add to the gall,
The club went farther than the ball.

Wishing On A Tee

My little ball sits on the first tee,
A wondrous sight for all to see,
So unaware of impending fate
To hook or slice or even go straight.

I swing at the ball with a thunderous swish
And then follow through with an earnest wish,
That where it will land everyone can see,
And we'll be together on the second tee.

Claude Schneider

Golf Score Epitaph

I suffered so much from scorecard errors
That death for me holds no terrors.
And out of habit I greatly fear
On this stone they've marked the wrong year.

I'm A Hacker! Who Are You?

(with apologies to Emily Dickinson,
I'm nobody! Who are you?—)

I'm a hacker! Who are you?
Are you a hacker too?
Then there's a pair of us—please don't tell!
They'll banish us for sure.

How terrible to be a hacker!
How to the public, you're a blight.
They shame your name the livelong day,
To anyone in sight.

Hit And Quit Golf

Into the woods my last ball goes
And where it lands, nobody knows.
With that wild shot I'm forced to quit
'Cause none of my group will look for it.

A Golfing Travesty

....

(with apologies to Michael Drayton)

Since there is no hope, let us putt and part.
Nay, I am done; you'll get no more of me.
Ask if I'm mad, yea, mad with all my heart;
You claimed a twenty and played to a three.

Shake hands, never! And cancel our tee times.
Be not seen with me on cart path or street!
Remind not the world of this day's crimes
And pray from the morrow we never meet.

I vow at the gasp of life's final breath
When, with pulse failing, passion speechless lies,
When faith is kneeling at my bed of death,
To never forget the scorecard testifies.

While I played the game in true honesty,
You claimed a twenty and played to a three.

Jillted

(with apologies to Mother Goose)

Jack and Jill were on the hill
To hit across the water.
Jack splashed his in;
Jill aced hers in,
Then tumbled down in laughter.

Claude Schneider

Down By The Thirteenth Green

....

(*with apologies to Hal Leonard Publishing
Corporation, Down by the Old Mill Stream*)

Down by the thirteenth green,
Where I first saw you,
With your balls so few
And you lost them too.

    It was then I knew
    That I must play through.

You took sixteen,
Which was obscene,
Down by the thirteenth green.

A Putting Prayer (1)

Now I stroke the putting ball
And pray the Lord that it will fall.
But if it dies before the hole,
I pray you give it one more roll.

A Putting Prayer (2)

Now I stroke the putting ball
And pray the Lord that it will fall.
But if I miss the outside break,
I pray the Lord my ball to take.

Golfing Hopes

Hope is the thing that keeps
Golfers coming back.
It overcomes the weeping
No matter how we hack.

Twinkle, Tinkle, Little Ball

Twinkle, tinkle, little ball,
To let me know where you did fall.
Buried in the rough so high
'Neath the trees that touch the sky.

Shine a light or show a spark
So I can see you in the dark.
Ring a bell to make a sound;
Then you will be swiftly found.

I won't leave you here to perish;
You're the one that I cherish.
Shine your light or sound your call—
Twinkle, tinkle, little ball.

The Final Resting Place

When at last my golfing days are done,
And the starter sounds the final call;
Lay me to rest 'neath the sixteenth green,
Surrounded by trees so stately tall.

It should be a grand and glorious day,
Many dear friends will lend a hand.
But if the service is like my playing,
They'll bury me deep in the usual sand.

A Disputtable Epitaph

Beneath this green
Lie the remains
Of one who died
From putting pains.

Thomas M. Edwards is a native of Milwaukee, Wisconsin and worked as Advertising Manager of the Buick Division of General Motors in Flint, Michigan before retiring. He now pursues his first love, writing. Tom specializes in amusing golf verse and is considered by many "The Ogden Nash of Golf."

Mr. Edward's literary achievements include: two first places, "Best of Contest" and "Writer of the Year" in Cookeville Creative Writers contests, two first places in Mid-South Writers contests, first place in Poetry Society of Tennessee, first place in Tennessee Mountain Writers, first place in Poetry Society of New Hampshire and first place in Roane State College writing contest, plus over 60 other writing awards. His work has been published in numerous newspapers, magazines and journals, as well as in the Town Spring Literary Collections by the Cookeville Creative Writers, Mid-South Poetry Festival Collections, Penorama, published by the Plateau Writers Group and "A Quiet Breeze" and "Southern Visions," both New South Poetry Chapbooks.

In addition to humorous golf poetry, Tom writes fiction, nonfiction, children's stories, and plays. He enjoys performing at poetry readings and is famous for his entertaining golf readings and story-telling sessions. He and his wife live in Fairfield Glade, Tennessee.

Order Form

If you would like to order additional copies of this book, please send a copy of this form along with check or money order to:

Raven Tree Press, Fulfillment Dept.
130 E. Walnut – Suite 410
Green Bay, WI 54301

Please send me _____ copies of **The Humorous Golf Poetry of Tom Edwards** at $20.00 per copy, plus 5.5% sales tax (Wisconsin orders only) and shipping.

Shipping charges as follows:
First book: $4.00, each additional book: $2.00
Orders shipped USPS book rate within 10 working days.

Sub total (Number of books x $20.00) $ _____

5.5% sales tax (WI residents only)   _____

Shipping   _____

Total enclosed $ _____

Or, you may ask your local bookstore to order it from our distributors.

We hope you enjoyed reading *The Humorous Golf Poetry of Tom Edwards*. Please feel free to contact us with comments, criticism, suggestions or conversation.

For Writer's Guidelines, send a SASE to Managing Editor, Raven Tree Press, at the above address.

Catalog available on request.